Snapshots

AF624656

Susie Brown

BookLeaf Publishing

Presentation by *BookLeaf Publishing*

Web: www.bookleafpub.com

E-mail: info@bookleafpub.com

ISBN: 9789357212205

First edition 2023

DEDICATION

For my Mum, Diana Roslyn Brown.

I Set Sail Today

I set sail today
In search of a distant star
I set sail today
In search of a new world
I set sail today.

I look down.
The water laps,
Smooth as glass beneath my metaphorical boat
An aquatic mirror,
Reflecting its shining images out into the
cosmos
I look up.

I set sail today
I float
Adrift on an ocean of feelings
Emotions flowing forwards
Upwards
Uncontrolled...
Like a balloon soaring gently higher and higher
Towards a new beginning

I set sail today
Embracing the peace of Spring
I give myself over to the journey
And take a breath
I set sail today.

The Contradictions of Me

I'm not a swimmer
But I love the ocean

I'm not a gym junkie
But I love Pilates

I'm not a morning person
But I love a sunrise

I'm not an extrovert
But I love performing

I'm not a drinker
But I love a gin

I'm not a cook
But I like recipes

I'm not a church goer
But I think I'm spiritual

I hate change
But I've coped with it

I'm not a mother
But I love children

I'm a mess of contradictions
But that's ok

Administration of Death

We're so very sorry for your sad loss

Burial or cremation?

We're so very sorry for your loss

Cardboard, MDF, Rosewood or wicker coffin?

We're so sorry for your loss

Hearse or van?

We're so sorry

This figure is for the rental of the refrigerated space

For your loss

Do you want a viewing?

So sorry

Notice in the paper?

Your loss

Do you have a celebrant?

Sorry

Can you have the flowers delivered to us please?

Loss

Payment is due in advance

May she rest in peace

Sign here

Time Passes - for Mum

29 days ago, I whispered to you.
Thanked you for loving me.
Promised to look after everyone.
You didn't open your eyes.
But maybe you heard.

28 days ago, you left us.
672 hours ago.
Over 40 thousand minutes ago.
Over 2 million seconds.
It seems like an eternity
And no time at all.

28 days ago, I said goodbye.
672 hours.
Over 40 thousand minutes ago, I touched your hand.
Over 2 million seconds ago, I kissed your forehead.
It seems like an eternity
And no time at all.

28 days ago, it was warm.
We sat together.
We talked a bit.
Did you hear us?

Today it was warm too.
We sat together.
We talked a bit.
Did you see us?

Now, there will only be days without you.
Hundreds of hours.
Thousands of minutes.
Millions of seconds.
It will seem like an eternity.
And no time at all.

But I like to think
That as we spend that passing time
We will still sit together
And talk together of you
And you will see and hear.

Tell Me a Story

Tell me a story
Sad, poignant, emotional
Let me share your pain

Tell me a story
Romantic, happy, heartfelt
Let me share your love

Tell me a story
Scary, suspenseful, eerie
Let me share your fear

Tell me a story
Funny, lighthearted, silly
Let me share your laughter

Tell me a story
Personal, memorable, special
Let me share your world

Ant Magic - for Dad

When I was little and I got upset
You would do something I'll never forget
You'd take my hand and you'd lead me away
"Come and we'll look at the ants," you would say.
And so we would sit and we'd watch the ants run
Zigging and zagging their way in the sun
And somehow my worries would run away too
Though I think it was just because I was with you.

When I grew older I still turned to you
When I worried and didn't know what I should do.
"I need to look at the ants," I would say
And you'd still take my hand and you'd lead me away
Not in the literal sense any more
These ants were imagined, but still knew the score
They zigged and they zagged just the same in my mind
While you shared your counsel
So gentle and kind
And somehow my worries would lessen in size

Because of your love
That was constant and wise.

Now you are older with problems so vast
They challenge the way things were solved in the past
We've still seen some ants
When we go for a walk
That have zigged and have zagged
While we sit down and talk

But oh!
How I wish we were back in the day
When looking at ants sent our problems away
I wish I could fix yours
But all I can do
Is to spend as much time
As I can here with you.
And hope that my presence
Will help you to see
How much time together
Still matters to me

And whatever the future will hold for us now
I hope, that as long as the fates will allow
There will always be ants
To zig zag in the sun
And that watching them scurry
Can still bring us fun

For whenever I'm lost and don't know what to do
Just looking at ants will remind me of you.

VISITOR PASS

Springtime Sundays - for Phil & Chris

The ease of conversation

When good friends come to visit

The enjoyment of sharing a meal

While sitting on the couch

The joy of laughter

While listening to stories recounted

The promise of future catch-ups

Spent on other couches in other places

They're the best kind of afternoons

When time stands still and nothing matters

Except friendship and fun

On those Springtime Sundays

Pilates Gal

There's an oasis on the highway
Called Pilates Haus
I visit there 3 times a week
And submit to the mercy of the reformer

A machine of weighted springs and straps
Designed to challenge and bring satisfaction in equal measure
As slowly, very slowly
Exercise by exercise
It strengthens me in body and soul.

I never used to like exercise
I never stuck at it
But this oasis on the highway
With its smiling instructors,
Funky playlists
Beachy vibes
And mantra mirrors
Has changed my life.

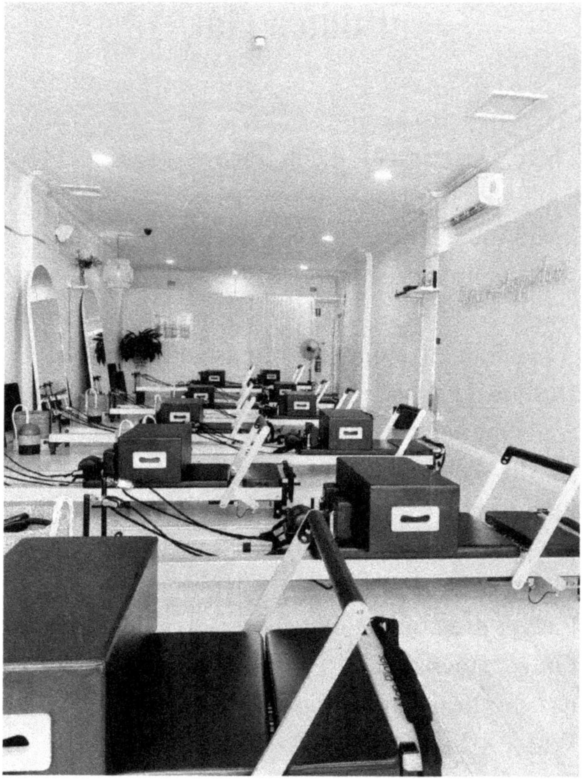

Netflix

How satisfying the background hum
Of streamed tv shows on repeat
A comforting nostalgia trip
For the mind
As the body sinks further
Into the comfy recliner
I should be working productively
In reality, I'm dozing happily
As the hours pass

I Bring You Love

Radioactive Mr Burns
An animated Simpsons character
Chock-full of radiation
Professed love to the masses
"I bring you love!" he crooned

Radioactive Susie
In real life
Swallowed radioactive iodine
For a hyperactive thyroid
Now I bring you love
From a safe distance!

Unplugged

TV, DVD and fan
Plug them in first, if you can
Next we add Apple and Fox
For alternative viewing "on the box"
A heater plug for Winter nights
And don't forget the pretty lights
Laptop, iPad, mobiles too
So much connection, what to do?
Will our power boards suffice?
(Extension cords don't look that nice!)
How much simpler lives would be
Without all this technology
But maybe it would cause more strife
To try and lead an unplugged life!

Cricket Tragic

I'm preparing for a summer
Of cricket day and night
Test matches, one day contests
And those fast and furious T20 battles

Domestic and international teams joining together
To bring entertainment to this happy fan
Sitting in her recliner
With the coverage in the background
Occasionally joined by friends
For evenings of camaraderie

Bring it on!

Spider Contract Subclauses

I'm not a fan of spiders...
So the huntsman clan and I have an agreement

If they stay up high
Still
Where I can see them at all times
Their existence is assured.

But...

If they move
Or come close to me
In any way whatsoever
They have to die.

Simple, yes?

Except...

When a small, 6 legged spider
Who is following all the rules
Chooses to be on the wall at bedtime
A subclause must be added
To the spider contract

I mean...

A sleepwalking spider

Creeping across my pillow in the darkness
Regardless of the number of legs
Would not be good
For anyone

Would it?

So Little 6 Legs is scooped up and tipped outside
Taken to its new home
By my heroic husband

I hope it is ok

I mean...

It had already lost 2 legs
And technically it hadn't broken any rules

But after midnight is not the time
To find a loophole in a long standing agreement

Am I right?

Young Mind All Grown - for Savanna

25 years ago
I taught a young mind
Who was clever and sunny and creative and kind
She always excelled at whatever she did
She was purely and simply a spectacular kid
And when she grew up
She spread out her wings
And flew off to do unbelievable things.

Fast forward to now
And that sunny young mind
(Still clever and sunny and creative and kind)
Has forged a career where she's bound to impress
Where her every endeavour will be met with success

Too old to sit now on that old classroom floor
Today she walked in through my open front door
For we now have a friendship that's destined to last
And we sat and we talked as the hours ticked past

School's (Almost) Out

It's Summer now and the countdown's on
Another school year has (almost) gone
But in between now and the very last day
"Administrivia" will get in the way
Concerts and yearbooks and parties and such
My little "to do" list is getting too much!
Tempers are frayed and stress levels are high
Last minute changes are met with a sigh
The finish line seems just a bit out of reach
I seem to have lost all my mojo to teach
Can I survive it?
Sure I can! There's no doubt.
Just a little bit longer
For school's (almost) out!

Listmaker

Gifts to buy
Events to attend
Jobs to complete before the year's end

Bills to pay
Goals to achieve
Projects to start and others to leave

Being a listmaker
Keeps things on track
Once you have started
You'll never look back!

Floreat Majestas - for Melissa & Antonia

I'm the eldest of three daughters
Separated from my sisters
By almost three
And almost ten
Years respectively
We are all different
But still connected

I'm the ambivert
Nurturing, an over thinker
Who likes control and hates change
Always wanting my loved ones to be ok.

Melissa is the complex introvert
With an amazing memory
Possessing inner strength and independence
And a love of all things feline.

Antonia is the extrovert
The social one, an excellent cook
A proud Mama Bear
And a fearless global adventurer.

As children, we made up plays and songs
And spent time together
As women, we forged our own identities
And spent time apart

But then reconnected
In times of both pleasure and sorrow.

My sisters are phenomenal women
And I love them dearly
Together or apart
We're living up to our family's clan motto
Floreat Majestas

Let Majesty Flourish

A day in the life of Aunty Susie - for Jack & Charlotte

"Aunty Susie, can you come here?"
"Aunty Susie, do you want to know something?"
"Aunty Susie, can you play?"
"Aunty Susie, guess what?"

These are just some of the questions I hear
When the niblings come to visit.

My answers are somewhat predictable
"Yes."
"Always."
"Of course."
"What?"

There's no greater joy
Than spending time with my
Affectionate
Curious
Creative
Fun loving
Niblings

Together, we are a
Silly
Noisy
Inquisitive
Imaginative
Team

I am smothered in hugs and kisses
And always sleep well
After we have said goodbye until next time
And the house is put back to rights!
I love them to the moon and back
And can't wait until their next visit.

I would have been a rubbish mother
But, if I do say so myself,
I'm a pretty awesome aunt!

May the odds be ever in your favour

Russian roulette
Is a needless, deadly game
Where players gamble
On an empty chamber
When they hold a loaded gun to their head
And pull the trigger

Covid roulette
Is a needless, deadly game
Where people gamble
On others doing the right thing
When they go out into the virus-laden world
Without a mask.

"We have to live our lives."
"Things have to go back to normal."
They say

But in this new normal
The cases climb
And the deaths continue

It's Covid Roulette
And I have never been a gambler...

So I refuse to play
And I wear my mask
Hoping that the odds
Will be ever in my favour.

Soul Mates - for Lajos

What a life we have!
Full of silliness and support
Full of laughter and love
Sharing coffees and conversation
Theatre and music
Hopes and dreams.

What a life we have!
In good times and bad
In stress or serenity
Whether healthy or not-so-well
There is always a cuddle
Or a hand to hold
Or an ear to listen
Or a shoulder to cry on.

What a man you are!
Loving and generous
Emotional and creative
Clever and funny
My friend, my partner
My husband
My soul mate.

Next to me, Darling.
Always.

Soul Renewal

There, on the shore
The silent mossy sentinels
Stand strong.
Steadfast against the relentless waves,
A carpeted causeway of beauty.

I pause.
Take a breath.
Smile.
Walk on.

www.ingramcontent.com/pod-product-compliance
Lightning Source LLC
Chambersburg PA
CBHW051747130826
49812CB00033B/1045
9789357212205